THE HEART LINE
METHOD

A Healing Journey That Rhymes

Poems by
ELSA BROWN

LEGAL PUBLICATION PAGE

All rights reserved. No part of this publication may be reproduced, stored in a retrieval system, or transmitted in any form or by any means, electronic, mechanical, photocopying, recording or otherwise, without the prior permission of the author.

This book is sold subject to the condition it shall not, by way of trade or otherwise, be resold or otherwise circulated without the consent of the author.

Copyright © Elsa Brown 2018

Elsa Brown asserts the moral right

to be identified as the author of this work.

Disclaimer Notice

All the healings included in this guidebook are complementary healing modalities and are not a substitute in any way for medical intervention. Please consult your doctor for any medical treatment and/or intervention and seek the appropriate advice. Thank you.

Acknowledgements

I thank the spirits of light for all their support and guidance in helping me to find my path and write this book.

I thank my beautiful sons, Richard, and Alexander, for allowing me to write this book and present it to you.

About the Author

Albanian born Elsa Brown is a researcher of love and light and a full-time author. She successfully completed her Biomedical Science degree in UK where she now resides. Her deep wish to clear the past, brought her to the point to find the right healing tools to follow her heart and to bring out her experiences as knowledge and wisdom. She practiced what she wrote and through this, she can truly help and support people who are stuck in their drama, to give them new direction and hope. Hope for people that they can change the way they are and be the best version of themselves for themselves.

CONTENTS

INTRODUCTION	1
I WANT TO	6
WHAT I DIDN'T HAVE	7
THE RAIN	8
DEPRESSION	9
MY DREAM	10
QUESTIONS	11
THE HAPPY LONESOME JOURNEY	12
HOW IT ALL STARTED	13
THE BODY PAIN	14
MY HEART	15
THE FIRST HEART HEALING	16
FEELING GOOD	17
I BEGAN TO FEEL	18
MY HEART WHEN IS SAD	19
MY HEART WHEN IS HAPPY	20
TRUE LOVE	21
I LOST MYSELF TO LOVE YOU	22
SOMETHING BORROWED	23
CHAKRAS	24
HOW TO HEAL	25
PRAY	26
EVERYTHING IS OKAY	27
BELIEVE	28

MYSELF	29
GROUNDING	30
THE FOREST	31
GOING BACK	32
INNER CHILD	33
INNER CHILD HEALING	34
THE LIGHT	35
MY HIGHER SELF	36
FRIEND HEALING	37
LORD OF AKASH	38
MOTHER MARY	39
WRITING TO MYSELF	40
FEAR NOT	41
FACING LIFE	42
I BEG YOU	43
SELF-HUGGING	44
HOPE	45
WATER	46
YOU DECIDE	47
AWARENESS	48
LIFE	49
THE SKY	50
NATURE MASTERS	51
CHANGING MINDSET	52
LONELINESS	53
SADNESS	54
DON'T GO BACK	55
TWO STEPS BACK	56
MEDITATING	57

THE SPIRITS	58
FEELINGS	59
HEAL ANY FEELINGS FROM YOUR HEART	60
ENERGY	61
ASK US FOR HELP	62
THE BODY	63
YOURSELF	64
WRITE TO ME	65
I WONDER	66
THIS IS LOVE	67
MY PAIN IS FREE	68
JUMP INTO YOURSELF	69
AFFIRMATION	70
GRATITUDE	71
CONNECT WITH ONE GOOD FEELING	72
TO WHOM IT MAY CONCERN	73
PASSING THROUGH	74

May peace rest in your heart

and in your world

Love Elsa xx

Introduction

About This Book

Through the many books from The Heart Line Method, I give people tools to heal themselves and hope. Hope that they can change the way they are and live a fulfilling life.

I changed my life through practicing how to heal my emotions, my inner child, my past and I found a way how to connect with my heart and myself. That brought me joy, peace and passion for life.

Through my experiences I bring you techniques and motivational rhymes for you to be able to change your life and live it purposefully, like you want to, deep down in your heart.

I had a hard life, I thought there is no way that I could change my life, my behaviour, my character, and the way I felt. I was feeling very depressed, growing up in an orphanage set me up to make limited choices in my life that I didn't want to make. To accept that all was my doings, was very hard and that is why it took me nearly ten years to heal myself.

The way it all started was because I wanted to have a better life, for me and for my kids. I wanted to be happy without having nothing. I didn't know how, but I wanted to find the truth, I wanted to find the light, to find love and most of all to have inner peace in me.

I left my masters as a researcher in pharmaceutical and biomedical field and I decided instead to became a researcher of love and light because I wanted to find out the truth. I became the hermit because I didn't want to pretend and lie to myself anymore. I pretended most of my life saying that I am okay, that I am fine and I am all right because I didn't know any better.

Every day was a day filled with pain and tears, I was crying for all my lost years and the pain that came with it. Every time I was healing a part of my body or my life, another bigger stronger pain would come up. It was ongoing, I felt hopeless. I thought I would be in pain forever and live the life that I didn't wanted to live, at least not in this way.

However, through the healing journey, I understood why it was happening and why I was the way I was. I learned about letting go, acceptance, forgiveness and that I am the healer of my body. I learned that pain is a sign of non-acceptance, I learned that forgiveness is the meeting of two souls and while it takes place the light comes in. I learned that when we let go it allows new opportunities to come in. I learned that dwelling about the past creates the hidden victim consciousness that we unconsciously build. I learned that ego is created by us unconsciously to protect us from the pain that others inflict upon us. I learned that comparing our life with others creates stress in the body which is the way to create inner obstacles and allow pain and illness to connect. I learned that inner peace grows into our body every time we stay calm.

There are so many things that I learned about myself and how to bring back joy into my life. Throughout this book, I have tried to bring you many motivational rhymes for you to take action to bring back the light and love into your life. The light is healing for the body and love is what makes life so divinely purposeful and beautiful to live with.

You will see from the many poems that I present that I talk about how life was against me, how I failed in life and love. How depression took over and how I overcome it and through these messages you can also find the solutions to face the challenges in a new way.

I learned that change can come through only when we want to and are ready to accept change. The negative pattern of inner thinking needs time to reflect and allow change to happen. Through time it does, it gets easier and through time the body and the mind heals.

We all need to allow time for the energy to do that. Energy is strong, is pure and is wise. We need to allow time for the energy to do what we asked for. Sometimes, when we ask for a wish, we think energy is like a magic wand and we expect for our wants straightaway to manifest. Energy is like a soup it needs the right ingredients for it to manifest and one of these ingredients its time. Allow time and patience for the energy to manifest. This time is also used to connect with our heart and with ourselves.

Connection with the heart and ourselves is crucial to manifesting a better life. I failed in life so many times, I didn't make the right choices, no matter my good intentions, I was always failing and I was depressed and very unhappy. I learned that I couldn't have a fulfilling life if I was disconnected from myself and from my heart. For me it was literally impossible. It is true, one cannot be happy while they are disconnected from themselves.

When I realised that, I began to work and collaborate with my heart and with myself. I began to heal each part of me and show commitment to my heart and to myself that I really want to have them in my life. I invited my higher self and my heart in my life. It wasn't easy to find myself but I did and that is what I bring to you throughout all of my books, a healing toolkit, filled with wisdom and many practices that works.

It is only through love and light that at the end I healed myself and through the support of the spirits who showed me the right way to heal and live life.

I begin my journey in this book contemplating about life, depression and the so many dramas that I wanted to know the answers off and through the rhymes I tried to bring in back love and light, to motivate you to reflect and to take action.

I bring these tools and experiences to you, so that you like me can find joy, purpose, and ultimately live the life that you truly want to live deep down in your heart.

I wish you a wonderful journey and may light and love rest in your heart

Love Elsa

Let the Healing Begin

Love Elsa

I Want To

I want to love and sit daily with my heart……
I want to live life and travel many miles…….
I want friends to light up my day…….
I want a day filled with fresh air……

I want to ………..

And that's how the healing starts
Wanting a better life

WHAT I DIDN'T HAVE

I didn't have the love of my parents
In this life that I live.

I didn't have fun or joy rides
to remember the little mini, me.

I didn't have a face to look forward to see
I didn't have me.

I didn't have nowhere to live
Just a place to sleep.

No one to talk and smile with
Just me, without me…..

The Rain

Rain, rain, little drops of heavenly rain
Creating a lake in my heart
Which is so hard to find.

I swim in the rivers of my heart
to heal the lost and afar.
Confused and broken
from the 1000 fake smiles
I swim in the rivers of my heart

DEPRESSION

I see, I feel but I am numb and blind
I live to breathe and survive.
The change is a long waiting list filled to heal the pain
Worth a while for a believer but not a human in unrest.

The sun is rising to dry my sparkling eyes
And here goes another waisted time.
Feeling lost till I find myself
Oh, my pain why don't you go away.

Hope to change, hope to live
Oh, my joy why don't you come for me.

Till then is all repeat, repeat…….

My Dream

Through my dreams I never dreamed
Through my life I never lived
Is time to wake and not repeat
The drama of my ancestors
That now I live.

I dream to see the unseen
I dream to live a good life for me
I dream a dream
Within a dream.

I dream now to be free……

Questions

I sat with myself and with the air around me
I asked what I didn't dare to have and feel.
I asked for change and a better life for me
   I asked to be awaken and to be free.

   Myself and the air listen to me
And that is how my journey begins.

The Happy Lonesome Journey

My healing begins
Leaving the jobs and few friends to see.
And with many questions in my head
trying to find a new mindset.

Many days to undo the undone
Feeling tired and unarmed.

Looking for wisdom to find myself
In this cold human race.

Loneliness now was my time and friend
To heal and rest my pain.

How It All Started

A few pains here and there
In my healthy body everywhere.

I feel the pain as needles in me
Trying to come out for me to see.

I denied my pain instantly
When I see
And that is the deepest regret
That now I live.

The Body Pain

Pain, pain everywhere
Why don't you go away.

My pain said to me
You need to thank first the painful me.

How I ask and the pain shows me
Surrender, forgiveness will bring healing to me.

Then my pain smiled
When I practiced all these.

MY HEART

I felt a needle in my healthy human heart
I felt I couldn't breathe
I asked myself what could it be?

My heart instead spoke and gently poked me
My dear I missed you
And the light in me.

Through me you can have everything
To see, touch and feel.
I felt my body cry
For the first time
Joyful tears for my heart.

The First Heart Healing

I sit and cry because I don't know what to do
Till now my heart was a taboo
I ask permission to come and be with you
And you open your doors to me
To be with you.

I look around and I see rainbows
Green grass and magical land
I see you my heart alive and as a being
I see you and your heart.

I said to you am truly sorry
I didn't know you were alive
I said to you that I am a good person
And that my intentions are good and fine.

I repeatedly said am truly sorry
And please forgive me
Forgive me my heart
And then I followed with I love you
While I sat in your arms and cried

I repeatedly said I love you
Till you trusted me.
Oh, my heart I missed you so
And I love you more and more.

That day I will never forget
How my higher self
Came and kissed your front of the head.
And gave us the blessing to connect.

That was one of my favourite days….

Feeling Good

I never thought
I could feel like this
So good and free in me.

This was the first time I smiled
Without something to hold and see.

Finally, I had a glimpse of a happy me
That was the hope I needed
To continue to heal.

I Began To Feel

Meeting my heart
Was all that was needed
To feel and see the truth in me.

How did I ever live without you?

I cried for you without knowing you
And now I know why.
I could never be fulfilled
without you in my life.

I love you, always my heart……..

My Heart When Is Sad

I made my heart sad
Allowing others to use her.

I made my heart sad
Through the many heartbreaks.

I made my heart sad
By not meeting her day or night.

By not smiling every day
I made my heart sad.

My Heart When Is Happy

I sat and closed my eyes
The full focus went into my heart

I ask her – Hey baby how do you feel?
And she shows me a calm jaded sea.

I smiled a thank you smile.

TRUE LOVE

True love is not a game or a battle
But a gentle look, a touch, and a kiss
And to find one
One must heal.

For those that rush into true love
That is what they will find, a rush…

The key to true love
Is to be open and trust
While you enter with an open heart

I say to you TRUST IN LOVE
And you say to yourself
I TRUST IN LOVE…….

I Lost Myself To Love You

I want to hold myself gently
Like when I was holding you

And when I do
The mess that you left
To be transformed into the love
That I never got from you.

I forgive you

Something Borrowed

Letting go is really hard
When there is no wisdom to find.

You feel if you hold on
It will come back to you threefold.

Nothing is worthwhile to hold
Until you learn to let it go.

All is yours anyway
But on loan till you let go and accept.

Chakras

Healing the invisible
Is really fun
Just imagine a colourful disk
In your tum

Spend time with it
Without asking for anything
And that is how you touch the past and heal.

How To Heal

I tried many things
But love and light only heals

When you sit with yourself
Let your feelings spread

Feel your pain, it's okay
Thank it that it's there

Ask for forgiveness
And say that you care

Then invite love and light
To live there.

Pray

It's good to pray everyday
Not only when you stuck in games.

Praying opens up the gates
Of healing your drama up to date.

Praying invites the light to heal
To rescue who you love
And those in needs

Praying is a must to keep
For a healing heart in need.

Everything Is Okay

Drama, drama oh poor thy
Why you always come to my

I come to teach you how to be calm
For you to have a restful heart.

Be calm no matter what may come
Watch your breath
for peace to come.

Believe

A believer
Is protected from hate and spam
To become one
One must have faith and trust

Believe in me
My better half
Everything is yours
No matter what you lack.

Trust in me and lean on me
I make wishes
Come true
Just don't try to control me.

Myself

I felt sorry for my self
And the lingo I used to express.

Your ugly, your fat
You're not good enough
Was all I had in my mind.

One day I see myself for who I really am
I put my hands in my heart
And I told her I care.

Since then
I am sorry, please forgive me,
Thank you, I love you
Is my lingo to this day.

Grounding

Grounding is nature everywhere
For me to be happy and connect

Connect with the beautiful me
Connect to be free

Walk and sit in nature
It's all it takes
For one to be able to connect

When you connect you will feel free
And full of wisdom and clarity.

The Forest

When I am in the forest
The trees call me
Come and play they say to me

Put attention in your heart
While you touch the tree
And that's how you connect
While all becomes a magical land

The tree sees the child in me
And says, hop in
Alice is sleeping
Use her key

Going Back

When the healing begins
Your mind will say go back
It will show you many memories
Some happy and others sad

Be aware of that and say
It is what it is,
look what is now
And exhale

Have faith in you
And live in the present
Going back is a game
No one wins.

INNER CHILD

My Inner Child
Was always sad
Looking from the dark windows
Of myself

I asked her to come and play
And she looks at me in dismay

I tell her am sorry and I love you
And she shows me a rainbow
For me to play

After the storm the rainbow always comes
Keep that my dear in mind
Play with your inner child.

Inner Child Healing

The truth is it takes time
Time to heal your inner child
I tried once and 10 times
But that wasn't enough.

I ask her what do you need
And she just looks at me

I close my eyes and see the mini me
I ask her kindly to come to me
I sit her in my lap and hug her
While I continuously tell I love her

And that is how healing begins……….

The Light

When I am sad the light comes
To embrace me

When I need something
The light comes and gifts me.

When I need a friend the light comes and listens
When I need love the light comes to me

The light is your friend my dear one
The light is your spirit team who always comes.

Trust the light
The body knows this energy
And they like each other
Said my spirit team.

My Higher Self

She has the pin code of my life
Makes my wishes and dreams come to life

She is always there for me
And always, always loves me

I call her day and night
To give me hugs in my lonely nights

To give me wisdom
To lead a good life
I call my higher self
Day and night

Friend Healing

When my friend
Asks for help
I sit and put both my hands
In my heart full of love

First I put my left and on top the right
I ask for my spirit team to come
I tell them help my friend
To cleanse hope
And bring her love

They smile
And say it's done its done, it's done.

Lord Of Akash

I meet him by pure chance
The leading spirit of Akash
With lots of patience and love
He shows me how to live life

To live life in the right way
No matter if its sunny or rainy days

I feel loved when am with him
I feel protected and full of dreams

Thank you Lord of Akash for coming for me

Mother Mary

Mother Mary comes to me
And brings gifts to heal me

To heal myself and friends
Through her light and all the rest

I feel lucky that you choose me
To spread light and healing
To all those in need

Thank you Mother Mary
For blessing me
With your endless gifts

Writing To Myself

I sit sometimes when am sad
When am sad and in despair
I write to my higher self
To support me and care

I write to her about my dreams
For the obstacles to end
And for a new life to begin

I write to my higher self
Because handwriting is grounding
And makes your wishes come true

I urge you to handwrite to yourself
For your life to change

Watch the magic begin………..
When you write to your higher self

FEAR NOT

I am scared of the future
I am scared to love
I am scared of death
I fear to be loved
I am scared to go out
In case my pain comes back
I am scared of people
They judge me always

I am scared of the ……..

Then the light came into my sight
And spoke to me softly and with love

Fear not my dear one
I am here with all my might
I will always love you
No matter what may come
You are a part of mine
Do not fear dear one

Facing Life

Facing life in the right way
Most have lost hope and sit and wait
Don't you know who you are
You are love and you are light

Don't be frightened to live
Don't be scared to breathe
Am always by your side
Even when you think am not

Live life my dear ones
Is one of my gifts for you
To love and have fun

Accept it my dearest ones
You are light and you are love

I Beg You

I wish for my dreams to come true
I wish for love and wealth
I wish for so many other things
I beg you to give me all and stay

My lovely one
You don't need to beg
Look inside you
What you have
You are the master of yourself
Remember that when you start to beg

Look into your heart and see
You have all that you will ever need
That is why you don't need to beg
When you go into your heart to stay.

I gave you all
For you to have
My dear one you don't need to beg
I love you always….

Self-Hugging

Hug yourself it's okay
There is nothing to feel a shame

Hugging is soul food
And eternal gratitude

You can say anything
Thank you my body
For carrying me around
Thank you for being you

Feel your body vibrate
Its ok to hug yourself
For the light to feed your cells.

Hug yourself
It's okay……

HOPE

Hope is a flick of light
Resting in your heart

Your mind will trick you otherwise
Remember to go inside your heart

Hope is for you to have and access
Allowing you to bounce back

Hope helps you manifest
When you want to create

Have hope my dear ones
Hope saves live's
And brings back love

WATER

Water is the medicine
That the body needs

When you say I bless you three times
It's light and love spreads in

Drink water consciously my friend
For you to heal and manifest

Through water consciousness spreads
It's another gift for you to create.

You Decide

Many may come into your life
Some will go and some will love
Some will hurt and cause heartache
You decide what is worth for kept

You decide to hate or love
You decide to feel the aftermath
You decide your inner growth
You decide what next may come

No matter what you decide
Do it through your heart
In there lies all your feelings
Of good old light and love

Whenever you decide
Connect with your heart
No matter what comes
Your true feelings lies inside.

Awareness

Being aware now-days
Is a must task to take

Awareness will show you
The bigger picture of life

Awareness connects you with yourself
And what surrounds you
Including the air

Practice awareness my dear friend
For a fulfilling life that awaits

LIFE

Have joy and passion for your life
Don't let others decide
Is a secret you must share
To play the game of truth and dare

Life is beauty and a precious gem
A gift for you to heal and have

Enjoy life my dear ones
Is my gift for all I love

The Sky

The sky is blue and sometimes grey
No matter what I am always there

If you look up above
You will see me dancing as light

Come and say hello to me
For your vibration to increase

Then the next day come and see me
To create and manifest

Come and say hello to me
You are my everything

You are not alone but with me
No matter if you see me or feel

I love you always

Nature Masters

You can pick and choose a tree
It is waiting for you
They are masters of healing and grounding
They are the healers for you

When you touch a tree, say hello
And stay till you feel the tree pulsate
It is connecting you with yourself
For you to be at your best self

The trees love and yearn for you
To be closer and connect
Go to the trees my dear one
For your thoughts to rest

Changing Mindset

My head is heavy and telling me
You are useless at everything
You cannot do what you love
Because you are not good enough

I cried days inside my heart
At how life is passing me by
I ask my heart what can I do
Looking deeply in the midst of blue

My dearest one you can create
A different life for you
If you change your mindset
Reverse it and cleanse it with me
Till you have all you've ever dreamed.

Loneliness

My heart is shinny and open bright
And is filled with smiles and love
On the inside I am at peace
And outside I am lonely me

Wisdom pours from my heart
To share it with someone
Many use a good heart
This good heart of mine

My heart comes to hug me
And I am no more lonely me
Say out loud she said
I love people and people love me.

Since then
I am no more lonely me

Sadness

I sit and with my heart I connect
I ask her why you feel sad
My sadness is my past
Not living the full life

I took a deep breath and
Forgiveness takes place
I am a good person I said
Whatever I done
I did it unconsciously
I am so sorry that I caused you that

My heart shares her pink light with me
And tells me all is okay my dearest me
All you need to do not to feel sad
Ask me to heal it and I will be there.

Don't Go Back

I feel sometimes going back
And old patterns come back
I worked so hard to change
Why do you come back

The light comes for me and shares
Wisdom, reminders and says

Going back, it delays
Your happiness and the good that lies ahead
Don't go back my dearest one
Keep up hope
And shine your light

You will find that going back
Your good future is at stake.

Two Steps Back

As soon As I have the ducks in row
Life takes me two steps back
That fills me with sadness
And lack of confidence

I ask the air what else is there
For me to do
Is it ever going to end
Or to be good enough for you

The air hugs me and says, I hear you
The back steps are for you

To grow the consciousness
That we all share

Meditating

Meditation is hard
With so many distraction in sight
I want to have a clear mind
To be the free spirit that I lack

I Watch my breath but my head gets tense
I watch my feeling but my thoughts interfere
I go back into my breath
but my head gets in the way

Then I finally found out
That is the grounding that I lack
Also keep your feelings in check
And find out how to destress

That is all my friend…….

The Spirits

Spirits are high vibrational field
For them to come
You need joy and to be still

Spirits can help you in two ways
To remove obstacles and
The big picture for you to see

Call for your spirit team
Is okay to feel their need

Feelings

All our feelings lies inside
Inside deeply in our heart
We can access them at any time
For us to live a blissful life

Every morning when awake
Call an emotion
To experience in your day

Feel its vibe and how it feels
For you to share and have
All throughout the day
With a smiley face.

Heal Any Feelings From Your Heart

When I felt angry
I verbally expressed how I felt
Fuelling the situation further
And both parties couldn't rest

Later on in life I learned
All feelings are in my heart
And to heal them
I just needed to go inside

I asked my heart, what am I angry for
And the anger disappear as quickly as a fly could fly
And that's how you heal all your feelings
When you put your attention in your heart

Energy

Energy is everywhere
Pure, strong and with wisdom
For you to have

Believing is enough
To change slightly your life

For anything to manifest
One needs to wish
And take action to create

The energy will help all of those
That believe and create

ASK US FOR HELP

The spirits are everywhere
For you to have and access
You just need to trust them
When you ask them for help

They see life in all its might
And have a different vision and sight
Don't you worry my dearest ones
They are here to help for you to live a fulfilled life

Trust and believe in them
It is all that it takes
For your life to change
Ask for us and we will help
We love you always………..
The spirits

The Body

Your body is for you to have
To live a life full of health
Your body is like a river
That allows life to be expressed

When you are in distress
You throw stones in the river
And unconsciously life changes its flow
And suddenly all is mayhem

Do not stress my dear one
No matter how it looks now
All is well
Let life flow and be a friend
Do not stress……………

Yourself

Far away and everywhere
Lives somewhere your higher self
She always love you
And is with you because she cares

We lost touch with our higher selves
Because we became unaware
Overworking ourselves
And making decisions through our head

Call her at the same time everyday
For you to reconnect
For a fulfilling life
That awaits.

WRITE TO ME

Maybe you don't remember me
And now you feel unfulfilled
Life is suddenly hard
Because we are apart

Have you noticed you cannot
Either create or manifest
Is because of us
Being so apart.

The solution to reconnect
Is when you write to me, everyday
Write to me my dear one
For life to be a joyful one.

I WONDER

Sometimes I wonder
What would happen if we connect
It seems so far away
Am losing hope and faith

My dear one
Keep your faith
Believe in me
Because I care

I will always come for you
Blink your eyes and I am there
Do not lose faith
It might be all a test

I say keep your faith

This Is Love

I sit in silence in my heart
I ask her so many why
She looks at me with gentle eyes
I feel that this is love

Every night I go inside my heart
Some nights I cry and others I smile
Sometimes I hum her a lullaby
I feel that this is love

My Pain Is Free

I made my life miserable
Hence it was very hard to heal
Each piece of me

I paid attention to each pain
By listening to its pain
I said none is your fault anyway
You are my responsibility I made

Focus on your pain and listen to its story
Do not judge it or force it
Accept it as it is
For the pain to release

And that's how you will be free

Jump Into Yourself

Jump into yourself
I heard myself said
I ask how and I listen in wait

You heal your inner child
Your past and your pain
Then invite me and never look back

Affirmation

Every morning
As soon as awake
Say out loud an affirmation
Of your choice
For you to create

Before any affirmation
Ask your spirit team to cleanse
The self-sabotaging patterns
For all your affirmation

So, your dreams can manifest

GRATITUDE

If you want to have a fulfilling life
Practice gratitude day and night
You can say thank you spirit for the light
And thank you spirit for the life

Thank you spirit for what may come
Thank you for home and for love
Thank you spirit for your support
Thank you for blessing my life

That's how easily gratitude is done
When you practice it day and night
Gratitude brings miracles into your life
When you practice it day and night

Connect With One Good Feeling

When I go for only healing in my heart
My spirit team said, where is the love?

I asked them, what else can I do
Connect with one good feeling
Came the reply

In the morning I go inside in my heart
Connect me with the feeling of joy I ask
I wait and I feel, so much joy in me
And that is how is done, is done

There are more than 400
Good feelings inside me
And Every morning
I connect with one

And that is how is done, is done.

To Whom It May Concern

Oh my, oh my
The timeless story of you and I
I write to you now and then
And you are always there

You are who I believe
You are my everything
You organise the energy
To manifest for me

Thank you spirits of everything
Thank you for being you
Thank you for coming for me

Now I write to you always……

Passing Through

Remember that life is a gift
To live as you wish

Have hope and believe
For your dreams to be.

Love Elsa

A HEALING JOURNEY THAT RHYMES

Welcome
to
The Heart Line
METHOD

THANK YOU NOTE

Thank you spirits	Thank you spirits	Thank you spirits
Thank you spirits	Thank you spirits	Thank you spirits
Thank you spirits	Thank you spirits	Thank you spirits
Thank you spirits	Thank you spirits	Thank you spirits
Thank you spirits	Thank you spirits	Thank you spirits
Thank you spirits	Thank you spirits	Thank you spirits
Thank you spirits	Thank you spirits	Thank you spirits
Thank you spirits	Thank you spirits	Thank you spirits
Thank you spirits	Thank you spirits	Thank you spirits
Thank you spirits	Thank you spirits	Thank you spirits
Thank you spirits	Thank you spirits	Thank you spirits
Thank you spirits	Thank you spirits	Thank you spirits

A HEALING JOURNEY THAT RHYMES

Other Books from The Author

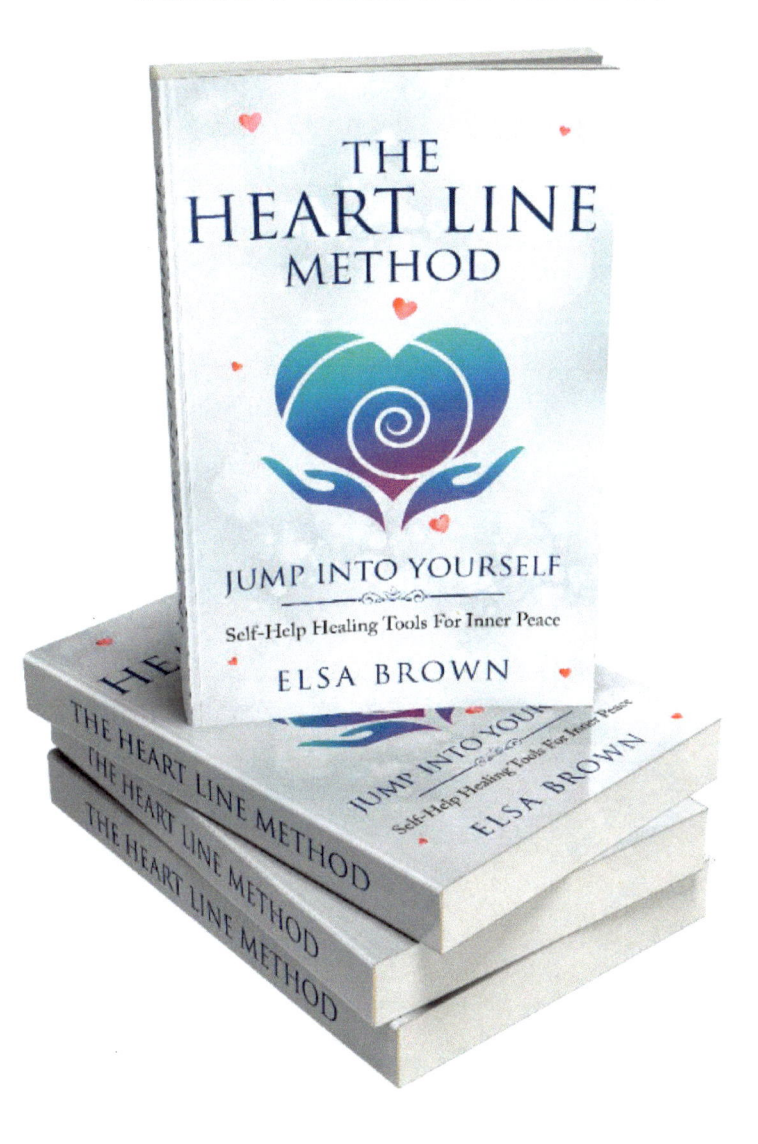

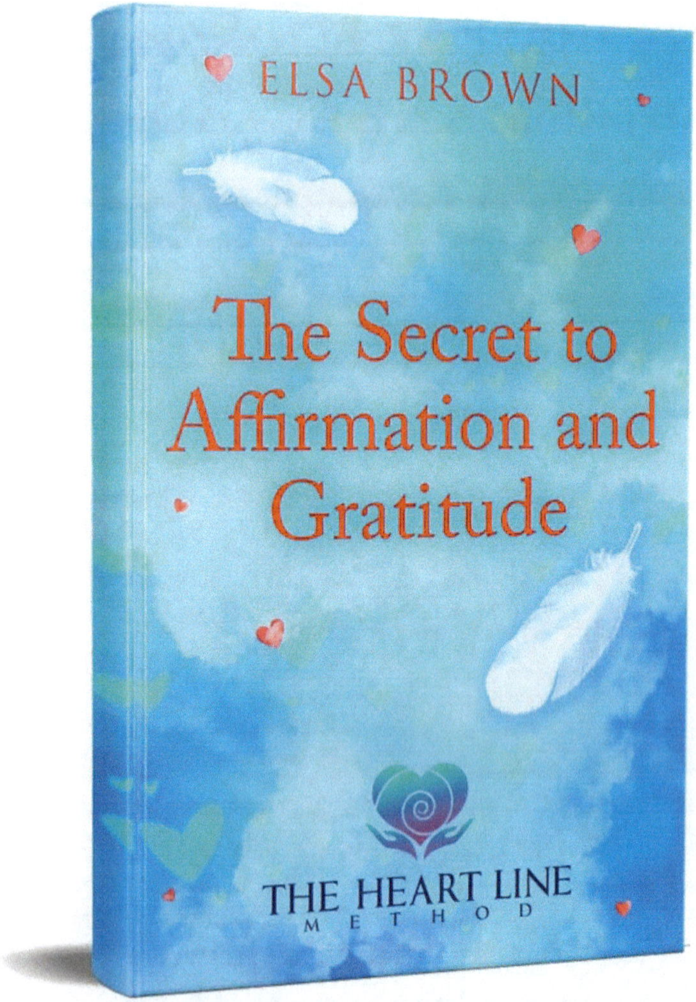
ELSA BROWN
The Secret to Affirmation and Gratitude
THE HEART LINE
METHOD

A HEALING JOURNEY THAT RHYMES

MANDALAS FOR MEDITATION

ELSA BROWN

250 Self-Coloring Mandalas to Relax

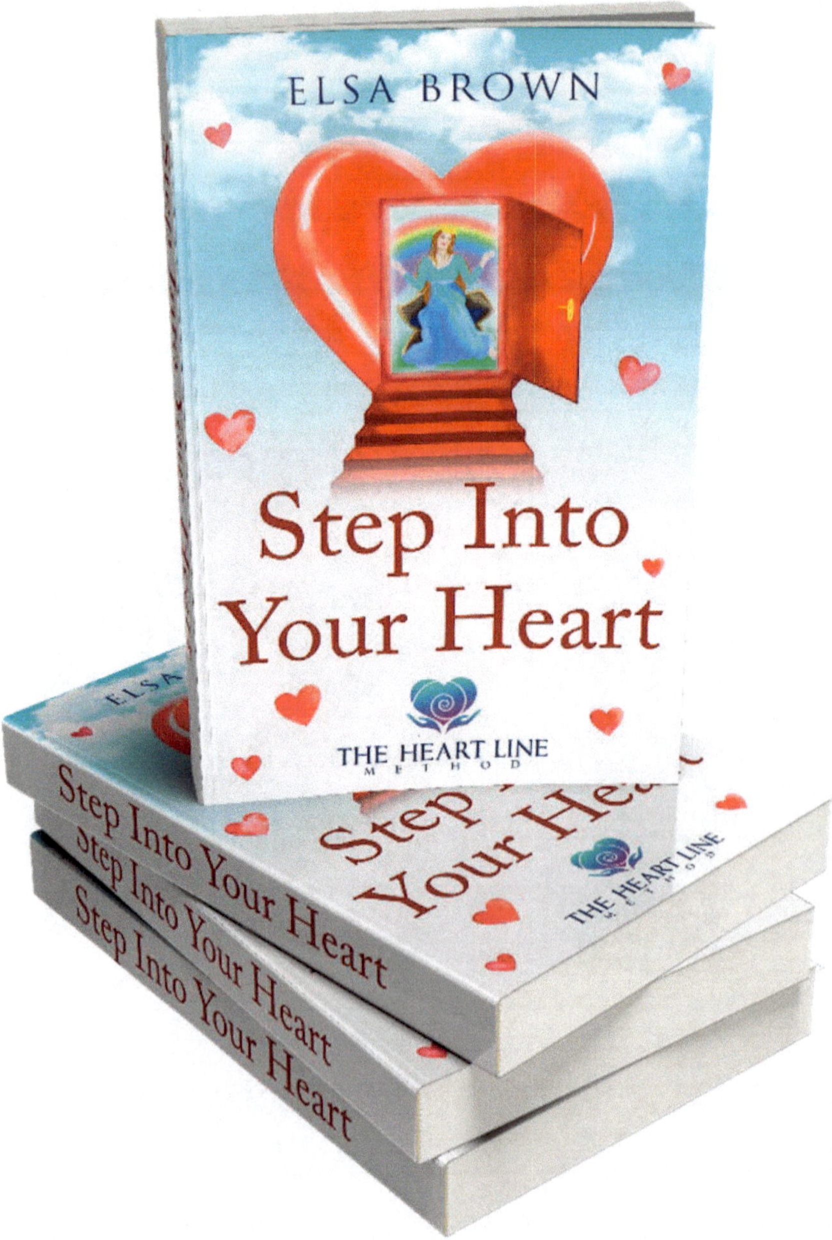
ELSA BROWN
Step Into
Your Heart
THE HEART LINE
METHOD
Step Into Your Heart
Step Into Your Heart
Step Into Your Heart

A HEALING JOURNEY THAT RHYMES

THE HEART LINE
METHOD

Soul Messages
to inspire you to take action

*Self-help Affirmation, Reminder,
Wisdom and Gratitude Cards*

ELSA BROWN

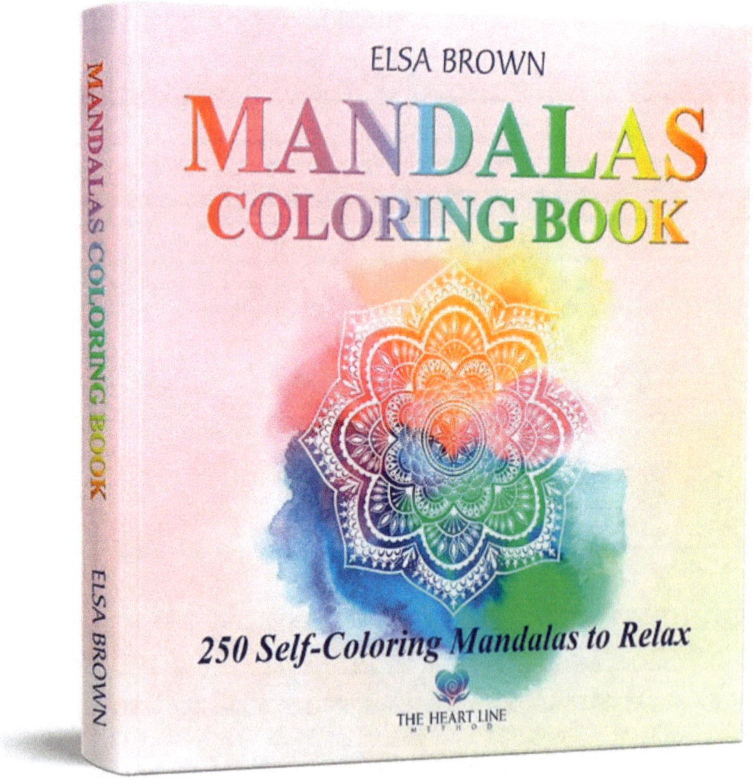
ELSA BROWN
MANDALAS
COLORING BOOK
250 Self-Coloring Mandalas to Relax
THE HEART LINE
METHOD
MANDALAS COLORING BOOK
ELSA BROWN

A HEALING JOURNEY THAT RHYMES

HEAL YOURSELF

Self-help healing practices for inner peace

THE HEART LINE
METHOD

ELSA BROWN

ELSA BROWN
The Way Into Your Heart
THE HEART LINE
METHOD
The Way Into Your Heart
ELSA BROWN

A Healing Journey That Rhymes

THE HEART LINE METHOD

Poems by
ELSA BROWN

Your Notes

A HEALING JOURNEY THAT RHYMES

Your Notes

Your Notes

A HEALING JOURNEY THAT RHYMES

Your Notes

THE HEART LINE
M E T H O D

Your Notes

Printed in Poland
by Amazon Fulfillment
Poland Sp. z o.o., Wrocław